On the Farm

This bo...

By Julie Ferris

Contents

Farmers at Work

Meet three farmers with different farms.
Don José is a sheep farmer. He is from Chile.
Mary runs a **dairy** farm. She is from England.
Ben grows vegetables. He is from the United
States. Find out what happens on a busy day
on their farms.

Don José Rajcevic is a sheep farmer in Chile.

Mary Mead is a dairy farmer in England.

Ben Burkett is a vegetable farmer in the United States.

Sheep Shearing

Don José is a sheep farmer in Chile.
He owns a flock of sheep. His sheep
grow woolly coats called **fleeces**
to keep them warm. Don José shears
their fleeces when it gets too hot.
Then he sells them to earn money.

SOUTH
AMERICA

N

Chile

**Don José's
farm**

Don José has
thousands of sheep.

Every day, Don José and his workers ride horses around the farm. They check on the sheep. Don José's sheep **graze** in the fields and can walk far away. Dogs help the workers to keep the sheep close to the farm.

a building on Don José's farm

Don José and his workers ride horses around the farm.

Sheep are herded into the shearing shed.

Sheep shearing

In January the weather is warm enough to **shear** the sheep. First, the dogs help the workers to **herd** the sheep into the shearing shed. Then the sheep are split into groups. Each group waits to be sheared in a different stall.

Each sheep is quickly sheared with electric shears. Sheep shearers are very skilled and do not hurt the sheep. They hold the sheep in place with their feet. Then they lean over the sheep to clip the wool.

"It takes just one minute to shear one sheep and six days to shear all the sheep," says Don José.

The fleece is sheared quickly without hurting the sheep.

The sheep wait until the whole group
has been sheared.

After shearing, the sheep are herded back
to the fields. Their wool is collected from
the floor and taken to the selecting tables.
There the best wool is taken away to be packed.

At the selecting table
wool sorters check
each fleece for
length and quality.

The best wool
is packed up in
wool bales.

Don José's wool is shipped to England, where it is used to make yarn, jumpers, hats and blankets. January is warm in Chile, so the sheep don't miss their coats. Each year they grow new fleeces in time for winter.

Wool Products

spun yarn	knitted jumper	woolly hat	blankets

When the wool arrives in England, it is washed, dried and dyed different colours. People make fabric and clothes from the wool.

Milking the Cows

Mary Mead is a **dairy** farmer in Somerset, England. She owns a herd of cows. Every day Mary gives her cows hay, grain and grass to eat. In return the cows give her milk.

Mary has Friesian cows.

N

England

Mary's farm

There is plenty of grass in the spring, summer and autumn. It is quite warm, too. Mary's cows go out into the fields to **graze** on the grass. There is much less grass in the winter. It is quite cold, too. So Mary takes her cows into a warm barn to eat grain and hay.

In the winter the cows stay in a warm barn.

Milking time

Mary's cows are milked twice a day. At 5:00 am the workers take the cows to the milking barn for their first milking. Each cow has a place to stand during milking.

First, farm workers clean the cows' **udders**. Then, they put a cup on each teat. This joins the cow to the milking machine. Milk flows from the cows through the hoses into big tanks. All the milk is collected in the tanks. It takes five minutes to milk each cow. About twenty cows are milked at one time.

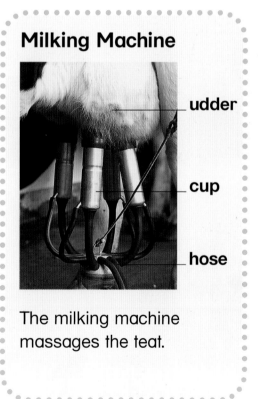

Milking Machine

udder

cup

hose

The milking machine massages the teat.

After milking, the cows go back to the fields. They walk around and eat grass. Then at 4:00 pm, Mary leads the cows back to the milking barn. There, they are milked again.

After the second milking, the cows go back to the fields for the night.

Mary and her farm manager check the computer.

Meanwhile, a lorry collects the milk from Mary's farm and delivers it to another dairy. Mary goes to her office with her farm manager to record how much milk each cow has given.

Milk Products

| butter | cheese | yogurt | ice cream |

Milk can be used to make many different foods.

Planting and Harvesting

Ben Burkett grows lots of different types of vegetables on his farm. It is in Mississippi in the southern United States.

"My family has farmed this land for 120 years," says Ben.

In winter Ben grows spinach and mustard. In the summer he grows sweetcorn, aubergines and peppers.

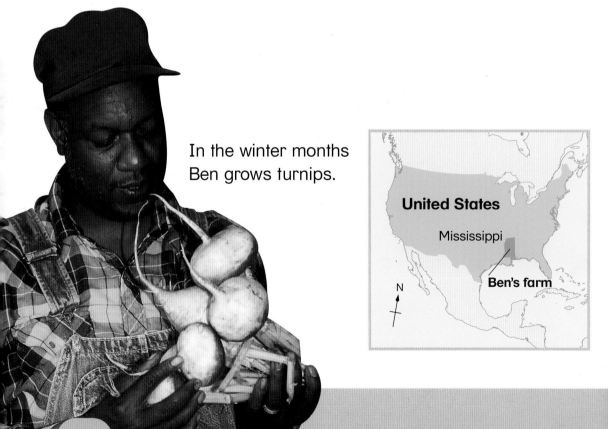

In the winter months Ben grows turnips.

United States

Mississippi

Ben's farm

N

Harvest time

In spring the winter crops are ready to **harvest** and sell. Ben and his workers go out into the fields to pick the ripe vegetables.

When all the vegetables are picked, the fields are empty. Then Ben goes back and **ploughs** the fields with a special tractor. He uses another machine to break down chunks of soil. This makes the soil ready for planting the summer **crops**.

Finally, Ben and his workers plant the seeds using very large tractors. Ben plants crops that will be ready to harvest later in the summer.

Sweetcorn takes eighty days to grow.

Ben checks his spring sweetcorn crop.

On most days Ben and his workers finish in the fields at 6:00 pm. But Ben still has more work to do. He collects all the crops and loads them into his van. Then he travels to the packing centre. There he unloads the crops and washes them. He packs the crops and reloads them onto lorries. Another driver delivers his crops to the markets to be sold. At last Ben can go home to bed.

Ben packs his vegetables into a lorry.

Ben's Vegetable Crops

pepper   aubergine   spinach   sweetcorn

Farms Around the World

Different farms can be found around the world. There are tree farms in Canada and orange groves in Spain. There are wheat farms in the Ukraine and tea plantations in Kenya.

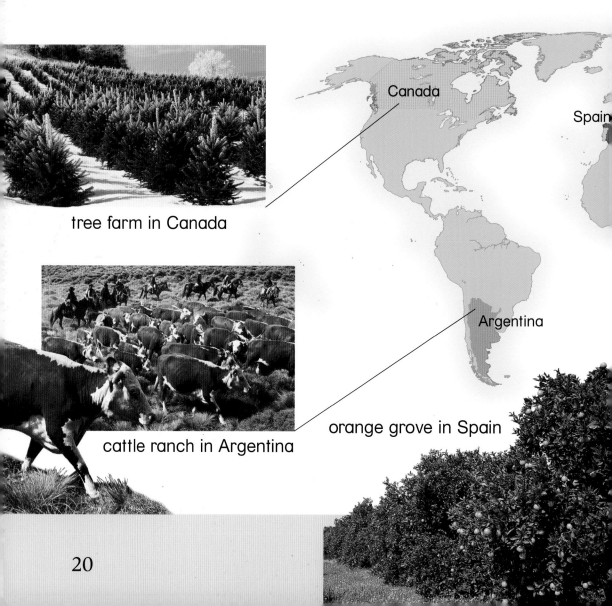

tree farm in Canada

Canada

Spain

Argentina

cattle ranch in Argentina

orange grove in Spain

wheat farm in the Ukraine

rice field in Thailand

Ukraine

Thailand

Kenya

Australia

sheep farm in Australia

tea plantation in Kenya

21

We have looked at three different farms in three different parts of the world. Don José looks after sheep and Mary looks after cows. Ben grows crops on his farm. Are there any farms near your home? What do they produce? Do they have sheep or cows? Do they grow crops? Perhaps you could find out?

Glossary

crops   plants that people grow and use

dairy   a place that produces milk or milk products

fleece   a woolly coat on a sheep

graze   to feed on grass or other plants

harvest   to collect grown plants

herd   to gather or keep together in a group

plough   to turn up soil

shear   to cut the fleece off an animal

udder   milk sacs on the underside of a cow

Index